Francis Frith's

Around
Luton

Photographic Memories

Francis Frith's

Around
Luton

Robert Cook

FRITH
BOOK Co

First published in the United Kingdom in 2001 by
Frith Book Company Ltd

Paperback Edition 2001
ISBN 1-85937-235-x

Hardback Edition 2001
ISBN 1-85937-352-6

British Library Cataloguing in Publication Data

Francis Frith's Luton
Robert Cook

Frith Book Company Ltd
Frith's Barn, Teffont,
Salisbury, Wiltshire SP3 5QP
Tel: +44 (0) 1722 716 376
Email: info@frithbook.co.uk
www.frithbook.co.uk

Printed and bound in Great Britain

Front Cover: The Town Hall 1897 39702

AS WITH ANY HISTORICAL DATABASE THE FRITH ARCHIVE IS CONSTANTLY BEING CORRECTED AND IMPROVED
AND THE PUBLISHERS WOULD WELCOME INFORMATION ON OMISSIONS OR INACCURACIES

Contents

Acknowledgements
Special thanks are due to John and Jane Creasey, and to Ruth Hall. I am also
indebted to Andrew Shouler, who once again has given me the benefit of
his knowledge and advice.

Francis Frith: *Victorian Pioneer*

FRANCIS FRITH, Victorian founder of the world-famous photographic archive, was a complex and multi-talented man. A devout Quaker and a highly successful Victorian businessman, he was both philosophic by nature and pioneering in outlook.

By 1855 Francis Frith had already established a wholesale grocery business in Liverpool, and sold it for the astonishing sum of £200,000, which is the equivalent today of over £15,000,000. Now a multi-millionaire, he was able to indulge his passion for travel. As a child he had pored over travel books written by early explorers, and his fancy and imagination had been stirred by family holidays to the sublime mountain regions of Wales and Scotland. 'What a land of spirit-stirring and enriching scenes and places!' he had written. He was to return to these scenes of grandeur in later years to 'recapture the thousands of vivid and tender memories', but with a different purpose. Now in his thirties, and captivated by the new science of photography, Frith set out on a series of pioneering journeys to the Nile regions that occupied him from 1856 until 1860.

Intrigue and Adventure

He took with him on his travels a specially-designed wicker carriage that acted as both dark-room and sleeping chamber. These far-flung journeys were packed with intrigue and adventure. In his life story, written when he was sixty-three, Frith tells of being held captive by bandits, and of fighting 'an awful midnight battle to the very point of surrender with a deadly pack of hungry, wild dogs'. Sporting flowing Arab costume, Frith arrived at Akaba by camel seventy years before Lawrence, where he encountered 'desert princes and rival sheikhs, blazing with jewel-hilted swords'.

During these extraordinary adventures he was assiduously exploring the desert regions bordering the Nile and patiently recording the antiquities and peoples with his camera. He was the first photographer to venture beyond the sixth cataract. Africa was still the mysterious 'Dark Continent', and Stanley and Livingstone's historic meeting was a decade into the future. The conditions for picture taking confound belief. He laboured for hours in his wicker dark-room in the sweltering heat of the desert, while the volatile chemicals fizzed dangerously in their trays. Often he was forced to work in remote tombs and caves where conditions were cooler. Back in London he exhibited his photographs and was 'rapturously cheered' by members of the Royal Society. His reputation as a photographer was made overnight. An eminent modern historian has likened their impact on the population of the time to that on our own generation of the first photographs taken on the surface of the moon.

Venture of a Life-Time

Characteristically, Frith quickly spotted the opportunity to create a new business as a specialist publisher of photographs. He lived in an era of immense and sometimes violent change. For the poor in the early part of Victoria's reign work was a drudge and the hours long, and people had precious little free time to enjoy themselves. Most had no transport other than a cart or gig at their disposal, and had not travelled far beyond the boundaries of their own town or village. However,

by the 1870s, the railways had threaded their way across the country, and Bank Holidays and half-day Saturdays had been made obligatory by Act of Parliament. All of a sudden the ordinary working man and his family were able to enjoy days out and see a little more of the world.

With characteristic business acumen, Francis Frith foresaw that these new tourists would enjoy having souvenirs to commemorate their days out. In 1860 he married Mary Ann Rosling and set out with the intention of photographing every city, town and village in Britain. For the next thirty years he travelled the country by train and by pony and trap, producing fine photographs of seaside resorts and beauty spots that were keenly bought by millions of Victorians. These prints were painstakingly pasted into family albums and pored over during the dark nights of winter, rekindling precious memories of summer excursions.

The Rise of Frith & Co

Frith's studio was soon supplying retail shops all over the country. To meet the demand he gathered about him a small team of photographers, and published the work of independent artist-photographers of the calibre of Roger Fenton and Francis Bedford. In order to gain some understanding of the scale of Frith's business one only has to look at the catalogue issued by Frith & Co in 1886: it runs to some 670 pages, listing not only many thousands of views of the British Isles but also many photographs of most European countries, and China, Japan, the USA and Canada – note the sample page shown above from the hand-written *Frith & Co* ledgers detailing pictures taken. By 1890 Frith had created the greatest specialist photographic publishing company in the world,

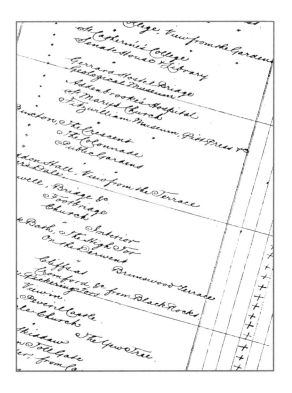

with over 2,000 outlets – more than the combined number that Boots and WH Smith have today! The picture on the right shows the *Frith & Co* display board at Ingleton in the Yorkshire Dales. Beautifully constructed with mahogany frame and gilt inserts, it could display up to a dozen local scenes.

Postcard Bonanza

The ever-popular holiday postcard we know today took many years to develop. In 1870 the Post Office issued the first plain cards, with a pre-printed stamp on one face. In 1894 they allowed other publishers' cards to be sent through the mail with an attached adhesive halfpenny stamp. Demand grew rapidly, and in 1895 a new size of postcard was permitted called the court card, but there was little room for illustration. In 1899, a year after

Frith's death, a new card measuring 5.5 x 3.5 inches became the standard format, but it was not until 1902 that the divided back came into being, with address and message on one face and a full-size illustration on the other. *Frith & Co* were in the vanguard of postcard development, and Frith's sons Eustace and Cyril continued their father's monumental task, expanding the number of views offered to the public and recording more and more places in Britain, as the coasts and countryside were opened up to mass travel.

Francis Frith died in 1898 at his villa in Cannes, his great project still growing. The archive he created continued in business for another seventy years. By 1970 it contained over a third of a million pictures of 7,000 cities, towns and villages. The massive photographic record Frith has left to us stands as a living monument to a special and very remarkable man.

Frith's Archive: *A Unique Legacy*

FRANCIS FRITH'S legacy to us today is of immense significance and value, for the magnificent archive of evocative photographs he created provides a unique record of change in 7,000 cities, towns and villages throughout Britain over a century and more. Frith and his fellow studio photographers revisited locations many times down the years to update their views, compiling for us an enthralling and colourful pageant of British life and character.

We tend to think of Frith's sepia views of Britain as nostalgic, for most of us use them to conjure up memories of places in our own lives with which we have family associations. It often makes us forget that to Francis Frith they were records of daily life as it was actually being lived in the cities, towns and villages of his day. The Victorian age was one of great and often bewildering change for ordinary people, and though the pictures evoke an impression of slower times, life was as busy and hectic as it is today.

We are fortunate that Frith was a photographer of the people, dedicated to recording the minutiae of everyday life. For it is this sheer wealth of visual data, the painstaking chronicle of changes in dress, transport, street layouts, buildings, housing, engineering and landscape that captivates us so much today. His remarkable images offer us a powerful link with the past and with the lives of our ancestors.

Today's Technology

Computers have now made it possible for Frith's many thousands of images to be accessed almost instantly. In the Frith archive today, each photograph is carefully 'digitised' then stored on a CD Rom. Frith archivists can locate a single photograph amongst thousands within seconds. Views can be catalogued and sorted under a variety of categories of place and content to the immediate benefit of researchers.

Inexpensive reference prints can be created for them at the touch of a mouse button, and a wide range of books and other printed materials assembled and published for a wider, more general readership - in the next twelve months over a hundred Frith local history titles will be published! The day-to-day workings of the archive are very different from how they were in Francis Frith's time: imagine the herculean task of sorting through eleven tons of glass negatives as Frith had to do to locate a particular sequence of pictures! Yet

See Frith at www. frithbook.co.uk

the archive still prides itself on maintaining the same high standards of excellence laid down by Francis Frith, including the painstaking cataloguing and indexing of every view.

It is curious to reflect on how the internet now allows researchers in America and elsewhere greater instant access to the archive than Frith himself ever enjoyed. Many thousands of individual views can be called up on screen within seconds on one of the Frith internet sites, enabling people living continents away to revisit the streets of their ancestral home town, or view places in Britain where they have enjoyed holidays. Many overseas researchers welcome the chance to view special theme selections, such as transport, sports, costume and ancient monuments.

We are certain that Francis Frith would have heartily approved of these modern developments in imaging techniques, for he himself was always working at the very limits of Victorian photographic technology.

The Value of the Archive Today

Because of the benefits brought by the computer, Frith's images are increasingly studied by social historians, by researchers into genealogy and ancestory, by architects, town planners, and by teachers and schoolchildren involved in local history projects.

In addition, the archive offers every one of us an opportunity to examine the places where we and our families have lived and worked down the years. Highly successful in Frith's own era, the archive is now, a century and more on, entering a new phase of popularity.

The Past in Tune with the Future

Historians consider the Francis Frith Collection to be of prime national importance. It is the only archive of its kind remaining in private ownership and has been valued at a million pounds. However, this figure is now rapidly increasing as digital technology enables more and more people around the world to enjoy its benefits.

Francis Frith's archive is now housed in an historic timber barn in the beautiful village of Teffont in Wiltshire. Its founder would not recognize the archive office as it is today. In place of the many thousands of dusty boxes containing glass plate negatives and an all-pervading odour of photographic chemicals, there are now ranks of computer screens. He would be amazed to watch his images travelling round the world at unimaginable speeds through network and internet lines.

The archive's future is both bright and exciting. Francis Frith, with his unshakeable belief in making photographs available to the greatest number of people, would undoubtedly approve of what is being done today with his lifetime's work. His photographs, depicting our shared past, are now bringing pleasure and enlightenment to millions around the world a century and more after his death.

Luton - *An Introduction*

'You must have been whisked here from paradise', said the silver-tongued Lothario in a seventies TV advert, to actress Lorraine Chase. 'Nah, Loo'ton Hairport', was her dampening riposte. Lorraine soon had her own TV series, and Luton went on to become the butt of bad jokes, suffering perhaps even more than its close neighbour Milton Keynes.

Plunging toward Luton today over the concrete carriageways from Dunstable, you can look down on closely-packed terraced housing, reminding us of a busy industrial past. To mark the future, there's a sign welcoming visitors to Luton and reminding them that this is now a University town. But some do not even take that seriously. Newspaper pundits have observed that University enrolments have dropped by 16% over 1999 levels, and that it is easy to get accepted here. But to put such aspersions in perspective, universities are encouraged to fight for their share of the government's expansion plan, and most are easier to get into. Meanwhile, a pub at the bottom of George Street advertises student accommodation. What heaven for the modern undergraduate!

So why isn't Luton heaven all round? Situated in a natural amphitheatre on a fan-shaped wedge of gravel at the northern end of the Lea gap, it has had a lot going for it in the past, and ought to have good prospects for the future.

The attractive countryside owes much to the Ice Age, when the glaciers' melted water flowed through the gap following a new course. The chalk hills, once extending further into the county, were eroded, leaving outlying spurs like Galley Hill. The Ice Age buried early settlement from a quarter of a million years ago, when people camped by the hillside lakes, surviving by hunting and gathering. Around 3000 BC, Neolithic or New Stone Age men arrived from France and the Rhine, bringing pottery, cattle and seed corn; they crossed the nascent channel on rafts. The Icknield Way, which connected East Anglia and Wiltshire, was an important natural (and dry) route for these early trading farmers. By the time of the Iron Age, it was a major trading route; people grouped to fortify hilltops, as territories were marked out for agriculture and settlement. Belgic tribes from Gaul invaded and made camp at Wheathamstead in Hertfordshire. In 55 BC the Romans came; their influence was all-pervading. They built Watling Street (now the A5) which cuts through modern Dunstable; south of it, where the ancient Icknield way branched to Luton, was the Roman posting station Durocobrivae.

The Roman occupation brought a long period of order. Then, as their empire became decadent, came decline. Picts and Scots rampaged across Hadrian's Wall, leading to the massacre on Galley Hill in about AD 360. Ancient Britons had the upper hand in the area for half a century; civilisation had to wait until the mid 7th century for Christianity to re-direct it. As part of King Offa's kingdom of Mercia, 500 acres were given to the Abbot at St Albans in 792, and a wooden church and bishop's house were built at Biscot.

The pagan Vikings enjoyed the church's prosperity and raided its treasure - the Saxons were ill-equipped and not disposed to fight. King Alfred did better than most, holding Wessex and making peace with the Danish king, Guthram. Luton was on the Saxon boundary with the conquered land, falling briefly under Danish law. Inevitably, the Danes returned to complete their conquest under King Sweyn Forkbeard in 1013, succeeded by Canute in 1016.

Further conquest by William of Normandy in 1066 established the nation's feudal pecking order. William's Domesday survey assessed Luton (then known as Loitone) at 30 hides, with land for 82 ploughs, 4 ploughs on the King's private land, 80 villeins, 47 boardars (cottars), 6 mills yielding 100 shillings, meadow for 4 plough teams, woodland for 2000 swine, 10 shillings and eight pennies from wood tax, and 100 shillings from market tolls. Leighton Buzzard, Arsley and Bedford were the only other towns in the county holding markets, and Luton's importance ranked second to Bedford.

Although still over 90% Saxon when William died, England was under the Norman fist. Henry II gave the manor of Luton to his illegitimate son Robert, Earl of Gloucester, and a new church was built south of the present St Mary's. Henry gave land to the monks to build a hospital and chapel on Farley Hill; another hospital, the House of God of the Virgin Mary, was founded by Thomas Beckett on a hill between the present car factory and Luton Airport.

Henry II spent much time in France, and his son Richard I went on the crusades. Richard sold the manor to a crusader named Earl Baldwin de Bethune for £80; the Abbot insisted on his right to maintain fairs and stalls in the market. Baldwin's 4-year-old daughter was pledged in marriage to William Marshall with Luton as dowry. When she died in 1216, King John forced Marshall to give Luton to his crony the illegitimate Falkes de Breaute, a vile man and a thief, by most accounts. De Breaute built castles at Eaton Bray and Luton. He also had designs on Dunstable, being a powerful man of many estates, including one gained from his wife in Surrey. This was Falkes Hall. Its name was corrupted many times until it became Foxhall; eventually it became a part of London, and was developed as Vauxhall in the 19th century. When damming the river near his castle, de Breaute flooded houses and stopped the Abbot's water mill; he could only wish he had waited until the corn was gathered so as to utterly destroy it. Out of favour with the new king, de Breaute met his death by hanging.

William Marshall's widow married Simon de Montfort, who led a rebellion against Henry III. He ruled for a year before being killed. The manor reverted to his father-in-law, the Earl of Pembroke. Life was harsh for the common folk, while the most brutal of their masters gained the best rewards, luxuriating behind the manor's drawbridge, eating plenty of pork, beef, vegetables, and bread and cheese, and drinking soup. The workers would have been clustered around in their cosy huts, at least when they were not slaving in the fields or fighting for their masters. Matthew Parris, a monk at St Albans in the 13th century, portrayed Luton as 'a place abounding with parishioners and richly endowed'.

Wooden huts fell prey to the fire of 1336, and the Black Death thinned the ranks. Harvests rotted, and rich folk suffered higher costs. Locals joined the peasants' revolt against 15 shillings poll tax, but Wat Tyler's victory was short lived; his rebellion was harshly put down by the young King Richard. But the ruling class would ignore this lesson at their peril. Parliament then provided no real democracy, but there was a local link with Thomas Hoo, the Speaker of the House of Commons in 1376: Luton Hoo, set in a 1600-acre park south of the town was the family home.

King Henry VIII did his best to force the country to modernise and cohere; he seized church property during the Reformation, but Luton had no monastery to dissolve. Serious trouble came with Charles I, who was determined to pursue Divine Right to the limit when he introduced Ship Money tax beyond the coastal ports. Parliamentary rights and privileges became an issue; the Civil War ensued, bringing considerable troop movements to the area. The king refused to accept defeat. His execution was considered the only solution if the rising, but rather austere, middle classes and their

leader Oliver Cromwell were to enact their vision for prosperity and rights in government. Restoration of the monarchy after Cromwell's death renewed religious differences, leading to the Act of Uniformity in 1662. With that came something to rebel against, and non-conformity was born.

By this time, straw hat making had become established in the south-east; there had been a steady import trade from Tuscany since the 14th century. In 1681 Thomas Baskerville passed through Dunstable, and noted that 'some people of this town are here very curious in making straw hats and other articles of that nature'. In 1689 Bedfordshire, Buckinghamshire and Hertfordshire straw hat makers petitioned against a bill favouring the wearing of woollen caps, saying that it would harm around 1000 Luton families. When Daniel Defoe toured England, he saw 'the industry wonderfully increased', and at Dunstable Arthur Young noted 'a manufacture of basket work which they carried to great perfection and neatness'.

Still aristocracy ruled the roost, and Luton's early Quakers had to be careful. The fearsome and unpopular Earl of Bute occupied Luton Hoo. Favoured by George III, he helped to break the Whig monopoly; he became Prime Minister in 1762, and in the absence of modern-day spin doctors brought the office into outstanding unpopularity when he concluded the Treaty of Paris to Britain's disadvantage. Hounded from office, Bute spent his wealthy wife's money extending the estate gardens

from 300 to 1000 acres, which became a bulwark against the town's southern expansion; he then retired to his other mansion in Hampshire, where he fell down a cliff while studying plants.

The Napoleonic wars and heavy import duties stifled Italian hat imports, encouraging cottage industry and the tiny straw-plaiting schools. The Walker brothers, Thomas and Edmund, also exploited the war by buying plait from French prisoners at Yaxley in the Fens. Peace restored the competition with Swiss fancy hats and Saxony plain straw, and falling prices meant destitution. Chinese imports were a quarter of English prices, and local plaiters could not compete with the machine sewing industry. Japanese imports after 1891 were literally the last straw. The industry collapsed.

Luckily, Alexander Wilson's Vauxhall Iron Works Co had outgrown its Vauxhall site in London, and by chance in 1905 moved to another area associated with its namesake, Falkes de Breaute. In the meantime, Luton had experienced modernisation in local government, with the Board of Health taking over key responsibilities involving water supply, care of the poor and a regular fire brigade. The first town hall, in Georgian style, was built in George Street; a room was rented to the Literary Institute, and other rooms were used for entertainment, meetings, the police and County Courts. A clock was added to commemorate the victory in Crimea in 1856. As further evidence of the zeal to improve minds, a corn exchange and plait

halls were built in Cheapside to rid George Street of sales. In 1882 a cattle market opened off Castle Street, thus clearing the way in Park Street. The provision of education moved from the era of generous benefactors and non-conformist churches caring for their own, to the 1870 Education Act, which was designed to produce more literate workers suited to advances in industrial methods.

Times were becoming more enlightened, but health care was minimal. Non-conformists believed that all would be resolved in an afterlife, but were often divided on issues of practice and organisation. The established church suffered declining flocks in a system which even to the uneducated seemed to be obviously run by the wealthy for themselves. Dr Thomas Peile had to modernise the parish to compete; he gave up much of his income to allow new churches in east Hyde (1859) and Stopsley (1860).

Luton joined the railway map. It was connected to London by a branch line in 1858 and then by part of the LMSR mainline in September 1867. J S Crawley was compensated for land lost, and bought that part of Great Moor isolated by the railway. As part of the deal, he donated land between Old Bedford Road and High Town, now known as Pope's Meadow, People's Park and Bell's Close. He went on to develop Crawley Road, Moor Street and Francis Street.

The town grew from 2,986 in 1821 to 36,404 in 1901, and therefore needed improved transport, among other things. The tramway opened in 1908; it was noisy and took up much of the road. The system was made obsolete by improved motor buses in 1932, but at the time it provided cheap transport for a growing army of workers. More new businesses were coming to Luton: they included British Gelatine, whose product was used to stiffen hats, Laporte Chemicals, who found a market for their dyes in the local hat industry, Davis Gas ovens, Skefko ball bearings, Commer trucks, and also Chevrolet/Bedford trucks following the GMC takeover of Vauxhall in the late 1920s.

With so many people flocking into Luton, the town needed more entertainments than the many pubs. The Grand Theatre opened in 1898, offering a fixed venue for visiting players and variety acts. Wardown Park was bought from the brick magnate Halley Stewart in 1904. The Council extended the lake for open-air swimming, and the park became a venue for fetes, where the first moving pictures were shown in a tent. A number of exotically-named cinemas, like the Anglo-American Picture Palace, would soon follow. Football was invented by the British working class, and locals proudly followed their own team - at the outbreak of war it was back in Division One of the Southern League.

Luton and District shared in the slaughter of the Great War (1914-18), and there were riots at the town hall when the peace parade did not offer room for returning soldiers in the official celebration. The

Town Hall was gutted, and the mayor fled in disguise.

If local government was still inadequate, there was no shortage of reformers. County Councils were effective from 1888; Luton's efforts to become a County Borough were frustrated by having only half the requisite 50,000 population for such status. The town did not even have a grammar school: the Higher Grade school could not meet the town's needs, and bright pupils had to go to Dunstable. Even in 1914, when the population had reached 49,978, Parliament opposed raising the town's status because the town had much of the county's population; the change would have meant duplicating services like education and raising rates for the rest of Bedfordshire.

World War Two brought a pasting as German bombers sought vital targets like Vauxhall (who were working on the Churchill tank); but more damage was done to surrounding property. Luton's Gas Company made tar for airfield runways, and the electricity supply struggled to meet the demand - this had reached 61,500 kw by 1945, despite strict fuel economy. It was economy all round: there were transport restrictions and the loss of the town's Greenline Coach service, because the vehicles were needed as ambulances. The corporation bus fleet was reduced from 64 to 21 following raids in August 1940, and vehicles were borrowed from Eastern National and Birch Brothers.

Before the war, Luton avoided the national unemployment misery drawing workers from as far as Scotland, but by 1939 there were 1200 empty properties. By 1945, pre-war house prices rose from £600 to £1000, and in some parts even doubled. There would be shortages for years to come, and utility furniture was the only style for the new home maker. By 1945 the Borough issue re-surfaced. The solution was to merge police and fire brigades, and delegate powers over education. The electricity supply was nationalised. By 1951, the population had reached 110, 381, but full Borough status waited until 1963.

Americans stationed in Britain during the war left a lasting influence and a longing for excitement. GMC executives came over to modernise the Vauxhall plant and by 1957, the new style was evident in the Victor and Cresta models. Driving was still a male preserve, and in 1962 'Country Life' advertised the Velox and Victor models as virile.

The 1960s were going to swing, and Luton was in the mainstream. It was chosen by sociologists Goldthorpe and Lockwood as part of a study called 'Affluent Workers in the Class Structure'. During 1963-4, they were testing the theory that well-paid workers were now middle-class. Goldthorpe and Lockwood looked at 229 workers and at a comparative group of 54 white-collar workers from Vauxhall, Laporte, and Skefko Ball Bearings. They concluded that the working man's social world was much more limited to his family, and that these workers lacked even the community of the more

traditional working class of older industries. They felt that the workers were involved in work mainly for money and what they could buy, and for the worker's needs, Luton had it all, including Europe's first Arndale Centre.

One reason given for the demise of Vauxhall at Luton is the industrial relations record of the Kempton Road plant. But wander round town today and read fly posters stuck on green phone cabinets, for instance, against the background of fading, crumbling and stained 1960s concrete, and you see globalisation and industry fat cats getting the blame. Workers rally desperately to protect their livelihoods, and the town's. This year's town centre Christmas traffic jams were weighted with old Vauxhall Cavaliers, symbols of better days, once gleaming and bought with factory finance packages, perhaps. Hats, hatch-backs - and what next for Luton? In 1997 both parliamentary seats swung to New Labour: perhaps they will shine a light. After all, the town has a delightfully multi-cultural community, which could become a model for the future.

Historic Luton

A THOUSAND YEARS of history cannot be accounted for in a few words, but we find hints of it in the streets today. Castle Street marks the approximate location of Robert de Waudari's short-lived castle, and is a reminder of the days when robber barons were inclined to cover the country to protect their gains and show their power. At Hyde, the Hoo was home to the powerful, and in the town, churches were built for the sake of a greater god. Along Park Road urchins posed for Francis Frith in 1897, and the countryside looked green and abundant. But idyllic thatched cottages were not then for commuting executives or media folk's hideaways; they were home to the hard-working and poorly-paid, who posed for the blanket-covered photographer marvelling at a wonder of science. The Parish Church of St Mary was rebuilt in the 12th century at a time when the feudal pecking order was well established and God's word was there to explain it all, via the elite who could read the good book. The church still displays design and architecture to marvel at. But most of Luton visible today is the creation of the last 150 years. Its municipal buildings, factories, warehouses, well-designed parks, terraces and tower blocks, bow windows and bays, glittering shopping centres - all are temples to the mighty necessity of consumption to keep employment and distraction going. All have grown around the centre, where only the wealthiest used to live, when transport was even more challenging than today.

The plait market used to be the centrepiece. Straws were cut to nine-inch lengths, bundled up and bleached, then dampened and flattened by rollers. Plait was brought from miles around to the market in George Street, where in the 18th century the county Quarter Sessions sometimes met in the George Inn. Straw plaiting was seasonal work and poorly paid; it has long gone, and we see a different world.

Someries Castle 1897 39715
Sited on the Hoo estate about 2 miles south-east of the town, the castle - actually more a fortified manor house - was built of Flemish bricks in the 13th century. Sir John Wenlock bought the manor from John de Cressy in 1403. The fortified manor house was started by Lord Wenlock in memory of his wife, who died in 1461, and was completed by Lord Rotherham, Bishop of Lincoln. Parliamentary troops were stationed here during the Civil War, and the novelist Joseph Conrad lived briefly at Someries Farm.

▼ **New Bedford Road 1897** 39729
The main road was diverted when Napier set out the grounds of Hoo Park. Leaving town by the line of the present existing Old Bedford Road, it crossed the river by a ford on the town side of Little Moor. A Turnpike Trust was formed in 1727, and the New Bedford Road opened in 1832. The road is very busy now, and the country feel has gone in the wake of developers.

▲ **Park Road 1897** 39726
◄ **Park Road 1897** 39725
In these days this was a country lane joining Trapp's Lane and the London Road.

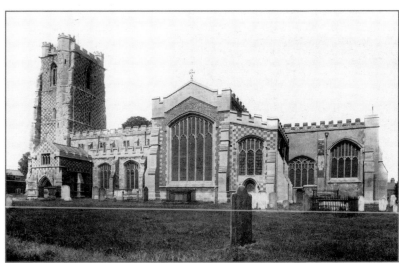

◀ **St Mary's Church 1897** 39706
St Mary's is a large Perpendicular building, which replaced the parish church in the 12th century when Henry II gave the manor to his illegitimate son, Robert, Earl of Gloucester. He demolished the old church, building this new one on 3 acres of his land possibly a little south of its predecessor. The work may have involved some craftsmen who had completed St Albans abbey in 1115. It is cruciform, 182 feet long; the width in the transepts is 101 feet, the nave is 40 feet, and the tower is 100 feet high. The fire engine was kept under the church gallery until 1864.

St Mary's Church The Chancel 1897

39709
The chancel has a mosaic reredos based on da Vinci's 'Last Supper', made in Venice and installed in 1883; the east window was rebuilt in 1886 by G E Street. Seats were provided for clergy during High Mass, under the abbot's coat of arms.

◀ St Mary's Church c1955 L117009
The chequerboard brickwork has benefited from a 19th-century restoration. Jane Creasey remembers St Mary's as a place for school carol services; she also remembers her organist music teacher in 1959-60, nicknamed 'Frankie'.

▼ Christ Church 1897 39716
St Mary's was the church for the whole parish. When Bute left the Hoo in the 19th century, the living was sold to various patrons, who appointed a series of vicars. These included Dr Thomas Peile, who surrendered much of his income to allow new churches to be built: East Hyde in 1859, Stopsley in 1860 and Christ Church in 1860. James O'Neill bought the living for himself when St Mary's had become run down; he remained for 35 years.

◀ St Matthew's Church 1897 39718
New churches were opened at Biscot in 1866, St Matthew's in 1875 and St Paul's in 1892. Another new church, St Saviour's, was added to Christ Church parish in 1860. O'Neill was dynamic at a time when people were drawn to non-conformity and the established church needed to appeal to ordinary people.

The Wesleyan Chapel 1897 39723
John Wesley was ordained a priest in 1728 and a missionary to
Georgia in 1735-7. He returned to become an open-air preacher for
fifty years. Never intending a breach with the Anglicans, he was
nevertheless met with hostility from Anglican clergy when he visited
Luton. They would not ring the bells or help him into his gown.
Luton's first Wesleyan Chapel was built opposite St Mary's in 1778.
It was used for 40 years, and then moved to new premises in Chapel
Lane (originally Hog Lane). Wesley had a gift for organisation: his
church encouraged the formation of branch churches. The aim of
the Wesleyans was to live the Christian experience.

The Waller Street Chapel 1897 39721
Non-conformist churches were schismatic over matters of doctrine and control. Baptists differ with their view that baptism is properly administered to those who have personal faith in Jesus as the Lord and Saviour. Their doctrine states that the church is a company of believers called out of the world and into fellowship by God. The first local Baptist Church was at Kensworth, drawing members from Dunstable, Luton, and St Albans under the leadership of Thomas Hayward.

The Union Chapel 1897 39717
Divisions among the Baptists led to the formation of the Union Church in 1836. Another split in 1846 led to the Ceylon Baptists' chapel in Wellington Street.

The Wellington Street Chapel 1897 ▲
39720
This was used by Ceylon Baptists who had split with Baptists after arguing over whether to pay a Minister.

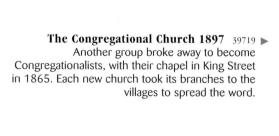

The Congregational Church 1897 39719 ▶
Another group broke away to become Congregationalists, with their chapel in King Street in 1865. Each new church took its branches to the villages to spread the word.

Luton Hoo c1955 L117050
The house was built to Robert Adam's great design, with gardens set out by Capability
Brown. Brown liked damming streams to create lakes in front of the main rooms; here
he made use of the Lea, which was widened for its passage through the park. The
house takes its name from the Hoo family. Thomas Hoo was speaker of the House of
Commons in 1376. The Hoo had been a separate manor in the 12th century. The
Napiers succeeded the Hoos; much later, the noted botanist the Earl of Bute - who
was also a discredited First Minister - spent much of his retirement from politics in re-
designing the gardens. After a severe fire, the house was redesigned by Sir Robert
Smirke. Another fire gutted it in 1843: the appearance of the house today is due to
the diamond merchant and royal entertainer, Sir Julius Wernher - Lady Zia Wernher
was a Russian aristocrat. In recent years it was owned by David Cola of Luton FC.

The Town Hall 1897

39702

Compare this image with photograph No L117088 (pages 48-49). The Georgian-style building was opened in 1847, a symbol of the town's growing status - the population exceeded 10,000. The clock was installed to mark victory at the Crimea in 1856. The building was gutted during objections to the proposed peace celebrations in 1919. Along the road to the right was the LMS railway goods yard at Bute Street. John Creasy recalls collecting train numbers, and watching trains thunder past to St Pancras in London or north to Edinburgh or Manchester. 'It was the smell, that was the thing for me', he said with a little irony.

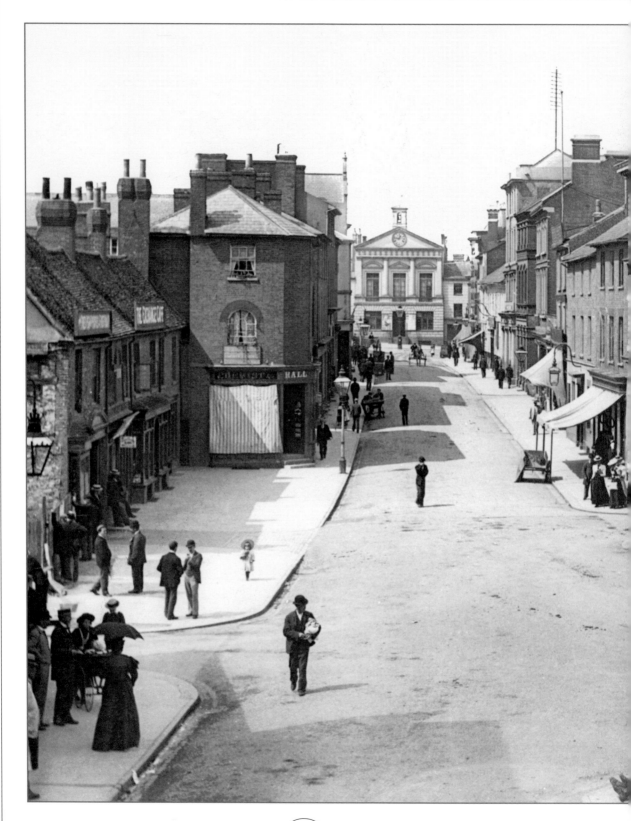

George Street 1897
39699
We are looking towards the Town Hall. The memorial in the foreground was known as the 'Pepper Pot'; it was raised in memory of the popular local man Lionel Ames. In 1869 the Board of Health decided to remove the plait market from this street, and built plait halls in Cheapside and Waller Street.

Park Square 1897 39703
In 1904 the town was pressing for Borough status,
and needed more school places. Temporary
accommodation was provided off Park Square until the
new building was ready in 1908. But this was a town
for working folk, and they needed boots. As we can
see from the shop signs, the square was just the place
to get them. Green's Brewery stood in Park Street, just
to the left and beyond Oliver & Son. There was a large
Irish influx during the building of the railway and later
of the M1. Duggans were a large Irish family with a
number of pubs in town.

Extract from: Park Square 1897 39703 (see facing page)

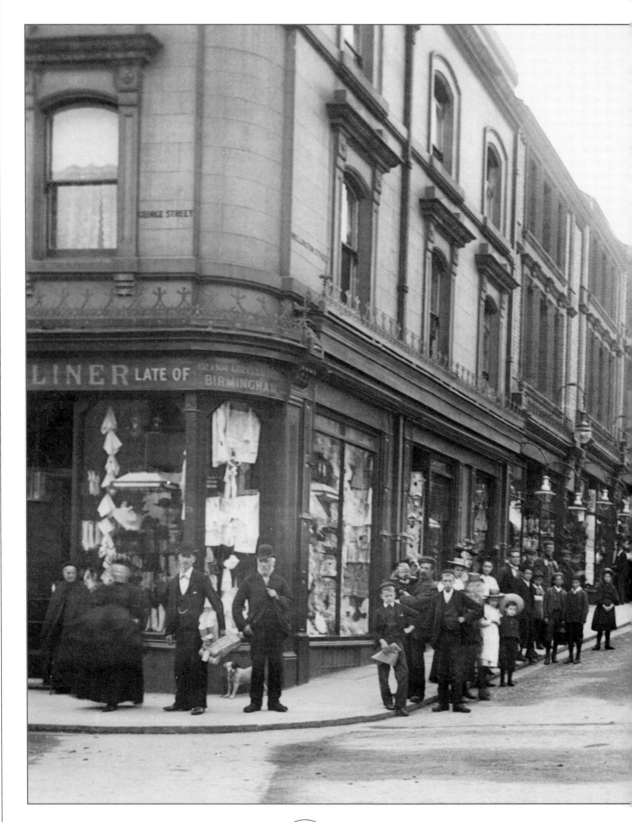

Wellington Street 1897 39704
This was the main shopping centre until the early 20th century, with few shops in George Street. The Wellington Cinema opened in 1912, showing a Saturday matinee. The shops are crammed with Victorian goodies; among them are a good choice of local hats. Jane Creasey, local inhabitant, recalls sitting on little wooden seats in Whites shoe shop, half-way along on the left, in the 1950s /60s. 'There were Startrite and Clarks shoes for sale, and children tried them for a good fit by walking on little carpet squares decorated with animal pictures. You could get handbags repaired also'.

◀ **The Bute Hospital 1897**
39713
This hospital proved more useful than its namesake! Medicine was still basic, and there was no national health service when this picture was taken. A century earlier it was even worse, with Dr Samuel Chase described as surgeon and man midwife. Good food from local farms protected Lutonians from the worst of wartime infections during the 1940s. Then raised expectations and a Labour Government created the National Health Service.

◄ **The Higher Grade School 1897** 39724
Bedfordshire County Council took over education in 1902, and it was hoped that the Higher Grade school would serve Luton's growing needs. At the time, boys were travelling to Dunstable, Bedford and St Albans. The new Luton Modern School opened in 1908.

▼ **The Children's Home 1897** 39712
These premises became a children's annexe to Luton & District General Hospital. Jane Creasey went there to have a squinting eye corrected in the 1950s. It has also enjoyed time as an Exodus collective with various escapist amusements!

◄ **The Wesleyan School 1897** 39722
Non-conformists took education of their children very seriously. Until 1870, on the other hand, the state did not take education seriously for anyone except the rich. Successive governments were eventually forced to realise that Britain would have no place in the modern world unless the workers were taught the 3 Rs.

The Entrance to the Peoples' Park 1897 39728
Luton has its parks to remind us of how great houses and landowners gave way to the needs of the many, with great estates being turned over to the people. No doubt there is more progress for the people on the way.

The Peoples' Luton

Luton was built on the leadership of some forceful and inspired leaders and the sweat and toil of working people who flocked in from far and near. Ultimately, as democracy took hold, it would become a town for the ordinary people, reflecting their fortunes in its ups and downs. Sometimes pride in a place can be misdirected, as one might hear from the rival chantings of Watford and Luton supporters at a local derby.

Luton's most famous display of public disorder happened after the peace treaty was signed in 1919. The Town Council announced civic celebrations to be held on 19 July, with floats, bands and entertainments for 9000 people and a banquet for the Mayor and Corporation; but there was nothing for the masses or the ex-servicemen. The council ignored protests, so the crowd marched on the Town Hall. They invaded it while the council was in session, drowning out the mayor's speech and throwing furniture through windows; they returned a day later to emphasise their point by ransacking the place. When the brigade arrived to deal with the resulting fire, the mob slashed the hoses; the hall was gutted to the sound of the crowd singing 'Keep the Home Fires Burning'.

Lutonians have also shown their mettle with some rather forceful responses to Vauxhall car management. Historically the company was hostile to the unions. Scottish newcomers during the depressed 1930s brought some passionate spirits. The management underestimated how much people expected from the post-war new order when they got involved in a bonus dispute in 1945. Trouble in the car industry reached new heights during the 1970s with a 3-month strike in 1979. This was a time of increasing Japanese competition; as Vauxhall was a fairly small design and manufacture unit within Europe, it was going to have a struggle to survive. A new agreement on working practices offered hope for the future. Sad to say, in the wake of local names Commer and Bedford trucks, the Vauxhall name is soon to disappear; but there is still much of good old Luton left from which new shoots can grow.

▼ **Wardown Park, The Flower Beds 1924** 75596
The park was bought in 1903 from the London Brick Co magnate Halley Stewart in 1904. At first the Council declined his asking price of £17,000, but the property eventually came via Councillors Asher and Oakley for £16,250. The purchase proved a boon for the town, though the mansion served little purpose until it was taken over as a museum.

▼ **The Lake at Wardown Park c1960** L117081
Bedford army trucks were tested here during the war. The local factory built a 4x4 giraffe version of the QL with its body on stilts to test a Ministry of Supply theory about wading military supplies ashore. This was superseded by the waterproofing theory, which was tested in this lake.

▲ **The People's Park c1962** 27608
It is peaceful here, but in September 1940 a German plane dropped a stick of bombs across Wardown Park, Wardown Crescent and the Peoples Park. Sid Creasey used to walk this way to work in a traditional ironmongers shop, where they had machines to trim the wallpaper.

◀ The War Memorial 1924
75591

The memorial proffers the olive branch and looks forward to a bright future. Definitely not expecting another big war, the town has cleared the site of the old town hall ready for something a little more modern. Meanwhile the local policeman is on the street, but there does not seem much to challenge his skills. F Merchant, the upholsterer's building, looks very solid and steadfast for the new age. The old library looks like many libraries did, with its little dome.

◀ **Production Line, Vauxhall Motors c1950** L117046
GMC executives came over from the US to get work back to normal after the war. Much of the firm's success was due to David Jones, the industry's longest-serving design executive. This is the L-type body shape, available in 4-cylinder Wyvern or 6-cylinder Velox versions. Both had the revolutionary rear hinged bonnet replacing the split bonnet. The Velox reached 75mph; the model ceased production in 1951 when it was replaced by the Detroit-influenced E-type.

◄ Vauxhall Motor Works c1950 L117029
The works are still wearing camouflage paint, having been a prime target during the conflict. In the closing stages of the war, a V2 nearly hit Commer Karrier's despatch shop in Biscot Road, destroying a house. The first daylight raid set fire to oil tanks, but did no real damage to the works. The greatest raid was on the bus depot, killing one and injuring twelve. Even Whipsnade Zoo was hit. But the factory continued producing the Churchill tanks, along with inflatable decoy trucks, decoy planes, side panels for jerrycans and steel helmets. Tanks were tested in the grounds of Luton Hoo.

▼ Vauxhall Motors c1950 L117028
During 1955-57 the company spent £36 million on doubling car production, excavating over 1.5 million tons of chalk and clay from the Chilterns to accommodate 1.6 million square feet of building. The spoil was used to extend neighbouring Luton Airport by 12 acres and to reclaim 32 acres of Luton Hoo Park. Steel work came from the US; it had been intended for a wartime GMC plant making B29 bombers. New block AA was among the largest steel frame structures of the day.

◄ Vauxhall Motors, The Canteen, Kempton Road c1950 L117034
The canteen resembles a cave, but in its heyday there was far from savage fare to be had here! In the 1930s there were 3 lunch sittings, and it was routine to have 2 pints at the bar. After the war there were no more production workers' lunch breaks or children's parties here, as output became everything. In the 1970s a worker told me that workers were so stressed that by the time they got to the canteen they would laugh at anything; he remembered them cheering if ever a worker dropped his tray-load of food and drink. All good things end: the canteen was demolished in 1991, and the plaque listing the company's war dead was transferred from within to the factory front.

The Library and the War Memorial c1950 L117026
Andrew Carnegie donated the town a library in 1910. A thirties Vauxhall 10 is parked by the memorial, and a modern L-type bearing the famous Griffin symbol is coming up behind the van.

The Town Centre c1965 L117098
This is the same scene as photograph No L117026 taken from a little further back. We can see that the 1960s have arrived with this modern shop and office block, which is housing an enlarged Boots the Chemist. The library could not compete with the confident stylists of this swinging age.

Manchester Street c1950 L117023
Here we are very much part of the busy centre. There are none of those quaint old poses seen in the earlier Frith images. The cameras are less obvious, and no longer amazing to these busy folk. The butcher's shop next to Shepheard's used to hang all their plump turkeys outside at Christmas. Two smartly-dressed ladies are crossing the entrance to Gordon Street where the Ritz cinema used to be. It is hard to imagine 1648 and phase two of the Civil War, when the Royalists retreated through the town to be confronted by the New Model Army at the entrance to Bridge Street in the bottom corner of this picture.

The Town Hall 1897 39702

George Street c1950

L117004

We are looking towards the white stonework of the Town Hall; only a few years before it had been in drab camouflage, because it was such a beacon to bombers. The frugal fifties have arrived, and the delivery van marks the location of the popular Lyons corner house. Here, ladies in little pinnies and frilly hats served the likes of Jane Creasey and her mum: 'I had a square of cake with little sugary bits. It was very dingy'. During this period, Lyons were notable for pioneering the development and use of computers to manage their corner house accounts and delivery schedules. The George Hotel held dances, though they did not encourage the local Teddy Boy element of the time. Dances were very popular with the growing Irish community. King Street is the turning just before the Midland Bank, on the left; this was home to the first launderette, where Jane Creasey enjoyed watching the washing go round in the Bendix machines for 2s 6d a time.

▼ George Street c1950 L117011

Blundell's department store on the right was very much like TV's 'Are You Being Served', with a man operating one of those iron-gated lifts. It was a rambling building with uneven floors. All went to make way for the Arndale Centre.

▼ George Street and the Town Hall c1950 L117022

This is a similar view to No L117004 on the previous page, but with a little extra interest for fellow bus enthusiasts: what appears to be a corporation-owned vehicle approaches the camera. The George has lost its sign. It is interesting to see the cyclists: this was clearly a time before mass motoring, and cars still had a curiosity and luxury value. Vauxhall and others would soon sort that out!

▲ The Town Hall c1960
L117088

The new Town Hall is redolent of 1930s municipal architecture, in a time when fear of Nazism seems to have been tempered by envy of Albert Speer's inimitable style. Apropos style, a locally-made Commer pick-up sits at the kerbside, while a raked-back Ford Anglia makes its way towards Manchester Street. This is another busy shopping day.

◄ George Street c1960
L117087

This is an interesting contrast to picture No L117004, yet it is still very much the 1950s; the High Street revolution has yet to happen. The American car, in the centre, could easily be a puffed-up version of the local Vauxhall Velox. The road looks quiet, but the hurrying schoolboy suggests something is approaching from the direction of the camera - unless the little scoundrel is just trying to blur the picture! Marks & Spencer is here, close to its traditional neighbour Woolworths.

▼ **Upper George Street c1950** L117005

This was once a popular location for solicitors' offices, and is still a place to spot the latest office girl fashions and to grab a fast food meal. The main post office and telephone exchange are visible in the distance. This was the way to the Savoy Cinema, where 'Davy Crockett' with Fess Parker was showing in 1953; Saturday morning seats cost 6d. Kids seemed more simple then, cheering the goodies and booing the baddies.

▼ **George Street c1950** L117006

Once again, the pavements are busier than the roads. The advertising on the old Corn Exchange, right, looks quaint. As the little van on the left indicates, these were days when tea came in its own special vehicle. The flower pots on the island really set the scene; they would no doubt give much pleasure if they were around this much-changed scene today.

▲ **The Corn Exchange c1950**
L117013

This view shows an old-fashioned Boots the Chemist before their move closer to the Town Hall. The first corn exchange was erected by the Lord of the Manor; he leased the tolls to the Board of Health who wanted the market off the streets as part of 19th-century improvements. The road here branches right to Castle Street and left towards the present-day University. Boots and the adjacent library were demolished as part of the sixties improvements, when glass and prefabricated building was fashionable.

◄ **The Corn Exchange c1950** L117007
We are looking down from the hill, with glimpses of the old Crown Inn and people taking their time about the day's business. Blundells advertise stylish furniture as the country moves away from the utility age. The Corn Exchange opened on Market Hill in 1869, originally for corn chandlers; business was done by means of samples. It was also used for public meetings and the Court Leet.

Castle Street c1950 L117012

In 1135 King Stephen was perceived as weak, and the barons decided to break their oath of allegiance to him. Stephen hired mercenaries to help him, and gave the Manor of Luton to one of them, Robert de Waudari. Waudari arranged the building of the motte and bailey structure that gave Castle Street its name; but the building only lasted 15 years. In this pretty scene, the Conservatives are still very much in control. But the empire is declining, and the common people will soon display their insatiable demands, leading all politicians into the nightmare scenario of how to be all things to all people and avoid bothering them with harsh realities. Not surprisingly, both Luton seats swung to New Labour, the masters of spin, at the last election.

George Street c1965 L117096
This is our final view of George Street - all is well. A Dennis Loline Corporation bus
bearing the destination Vauxhall Works approaches the island. There used to be a queue
of such buses waiting to take car makers home at night. Like the sturdy Humber Hawk,
Vauxhall looks like a name set to vanish from the once proud British Car industry.
Vauxhall never seemed to better the company reps' favourite, the Cavalier, and was not
helped by sneering reviews in the British media. Desperate measures to cut prices by
12.5 per cent seem to have done little good. The little street sweeper's truck and the
Morris Minor are also evocative of steadier days and of thinking on a smaller scale.

Stopsley
The Memorial c1955 S381010
Stopsley is a hamlet 2 miles from Luton on the northern fringe
of the Chilterns; it used to depend on farming, straw plaiting
and brick making, but signs of change are there in the
background with H C Janes office block. I remember working
for this firm as a labourer and dumper driver in the early 1970s.

The Secondary Technical School c1955 L117080
John Creasey, aged 11, was here in 1956. He remembers that during the first two years detentions involved picking stones from the field, because it was a mass of them and the pupils could not use it. Every day there was a morning hymn and inspirational talk from the first headmaster, Dr Charlesworth. John recalls that there was a rather liberal regime at the school. Luton schools were recently in the news when a local teacher declined to send his child to a predominantly ethnic minority school and was suspended from duty. There are considerable ethnic communities in the older terraced housing like Bury Park.

Stopsley, The High School c1965 S381002
One former pupil, who was here in the early 1960s, recalls that there was a farm area with goats, a greenhouse, and huts. On one occasion, the boilers backfired and they had to escape because of all the black smoke.

Luton Airport c1965 L117102

An Autair HS 748 is on the runway. The airport opened in 1938, on the 329 Green Farm site on the 500 foot contour, which limited radiation fog. During the war it was home to Percival Aircraft and 245 DH Mosquitos were built here. Autair were among the airlines establishing themselves here to exploit the package holiday boom. Dennis Elsden recalls his days with Autair management: 'In my first winter there was heavy snow, and Maurice Rowan persuaded them to bring a bulldozer off the M1. Bill Buxton was operations director. They used to drop a brick on a string from the control tower on to the roof of his caravan to let him know one of our planes was coming in. We had two Dakotas. When we took delivery of our second Dakota, Captain Maurice Rowan failed the port engine to check the restart, then he failed the starboard and it wouldn't restart. He called the tower for engineering advice, so they banged on the caravan roof, and Bill clambers up. As a Yorkshire man he didn't mince words; he said 'Say after me: Our Father, which art in heaven...' Those were the days when we had two hostesses and two pilots with weekend freelancers; one was Dr Kingsmill. We had a tragedy when a training captain took a pilot up to qualify on an HS125; he couldn't restart the engines after failing, leading to a fatal crash on Vauxhall Works. There were funny moments too. One pilot agreed to sell his stewardesses to an appreciative Arab, took the money and raised the crew early to do a bunk. Another chap used to joke when customs asked him if he'd anything to declare; 'Just the usual gold bar', he would say. This went on until a new customs officer checked, and found he wasn't joking ! We did well, but were taken over by Court Shipping line, who painted the planes up in exotic colours and expanded services, but we were brought down when world shipping brought down the group'.

Down Dunstable

The town nowadays virtually merges with Luton, but it owes its origins to its location on the Icknield Way and to the effects of the Romans building Watling Street; this made it an important cross-roads settlement. Ancient burial sites on the Downs indicate people were here long before. Inevitably, at a busy cross roads travellers once fell foul of robbers, but the town was well-established by 1119. The king founded the priory in 1132, and Dominican friars came in 1290 - the monastic buildings have gone, however. Queen Eleanor's funeral procession passed through in 1290; there was once a cross to commemorate this, but it was destroyed during the Civil War.

The town was advanced in public health, ordering in 1221 that butchers should not cast blood and waste into the street. Thus it was a good enough place for Henry VIII to hold his pre-judged divorce case against Catherine of Aragon, and in 1533 Thomas Cranmer pronounced judgement in church. The nation's needs were Henry's needs, so he accepted Cranmer's scheme to set up his own church and to confiscate Roman Catholic Church property. Closing the priory brought decline, and royalty had no cause to visit. The Civil War livened things up: the Royalists shot the landlord of the Red Lion inn because he refused them horses.

The stage coach brought steady through traffic and trade, boosting the fortunes of the Saracen's Head and other inns. The rise of straw hat-making really set things rolling, and the town became famous; but the population was still ▶

Dunstable, The Downs c1960 D69014
The downs are popular with gliders and courting couples. In 1965 Luton zoned the downs to exclude non-radio aircraft and the particular problem of gliders, which had become a nuisance to aircraft on final approaches.

only 4000 when it was incorporated in 1864, compared with Luton's 15,329. Like Luton, it grew apace between and after the wars. It shared in the fortunes of the motor trade as the home of commercial vehicle builders and AC Delco, who made carburettors. But in spite of all - the over-spill sprawl, the array of colourful shops, leather-skirted and tight jean-clad girls striding out of the hairdressers to parade along the High Street adding glamour to the densely-packed buildings, the re-locating industry - there are havens of history. There is the great Norman Priory Church, which must be the pinnacle of local architecture; after years of labour, it was consecrated in 1213. To the south are the downs, with splendid views, and the zoo is not far away at Whipsnade.

Dunstable, The Town Hall 1897 39738
A wayfarer either poses for Francis Frith or takes a rest. Perhaps he is waiting for the Crown to open.

Dunstable
The High Street 1897 39735
We are looking north. This is summertime, and the blinds are down to keep the sun off the goods, which are mainly of the necessary kind, like boots and shoes. The road has its share of horse muck, which enterprising lads will no doubt have scooped up for sale to allotment keepers or rose growers. This was long a major route from London to the north, and J B Hill's Family and Commercial Hotel would have done a roaring trade.

**Dunstable
High Street 1897**
39736
A substantial post office dominates the view. Ladies' fashions are very different to those of just over a hundred years later, when the modern female strides forward without the kind of dignified reserve displayed far right. How warm and cosy all would have looked under the dimly flickering gas lights fuelled by the new-fangled local gas works.

◀ **Dunstable, High Street 1897** 39737
This view looks north towards the cross-roads; the London-Holyhead telegraph poles are in situ. Urchins, horses and carts dominate the carriageway. London Central Meat Company have large premises on the left, representing the beginnings of the chain store movement into the area. Shop blinds sweep across the pavement, and the shadows show that it is quite a sunny day.

◀ Dunstable, High Street 1898
40956

We are looking north along the A5, with the Town Hall tower on the grey horizon. Tall telegraph poles carry messages the length of the nation, but technology is still so new and remarkable that the urchins here pause for the camera. The avenue of trees ensures that for all the demands of encroaching industry, Dunstable's citizens remain in touch with nature.

▼ Dunstable, High Street c1955
D69020

This is an interesting contrast to photograph No 39737, because so little has changed. Reams of cloth still shield the shops, and the traffic is so light that elderly pedestrians risk the open carriageway rather than use the zebra crossing - they obviously have not seen the leather-clad biker roaring into the picture bottom left. The coach reminds us that the A5 has much history as a coaching route; it is waiting by the 'no waiting' sign. Meanwhile, the London Central Company are still in business as family butchers.

◀ Dunstable, The Priory Church 1897 39741
The church is viewed from the meadows. It was built from the more resistant lower chalk or clunch stone, which is better known for its contribution to the cement industry. The priory held several estates in central Bedfordshire.

◀ **Dunstable, The Priory Church, North-West 1897** 39743
The church once had a central tower, transepts, a presbytery and a large eastern Lady Chapel, where Archbishop Thomas Cranmer held his court. The nave was parish church for the town.

**Dunstable
The Priory Church
1897** 39746
Here we see the Priory's beautifully carved Norman doorway into which a later door has been set. The canons of Dunstable were keen sheep farmers, with flocks on the downs where the road leads off to Aylesbury.

**Dunstable ▶
The Priory Church
Interior 1897** 39749
A gallery of seven Early English lancets runs along the west wall.

◀ **Dunstable, The Priory Church, West Front c1955** D69012
Here the church looks serene, but nowadays it is a little marooned by the traffic flow. The building has a lop-sided look, having originally had two great towers until both came crashing down in a storm in 1222. It was not until the 15th century that the tower here was rebuilt.

Dunstable, West Street 1898 40957
We are near the junction named after the nation's favourite Queen, Victoria. The boy is reading something gripping, perhaps a penny dreadful. Parked carts on the pavement look a little more attractive than today's cars littering everywhere, and traffic pollution is nothing worse than a few horse droppings! Under the shop awning, a long-aproned lady chats to a man in a wheel chair - perhaps a war veteran from some Imperial conflict.

◀ **Dunstable, The Grammar School 1897** 39739
The Grammar School opened in 1888. The headmaster, L C Thring and the school were very much part of the community, and traditional features like founders' day and speech day were important local events. Those wer the days before political correctness and school marketing Schools like this were not afraid to teach character.

◄ Dunstable
West Street 1924

75582

There are signs of a little Royalist celebration - perhaps it is Empire Day! Where's the street party? West Street led up to the Downs and Whipsnade, home of the famous Zoo since the 1930s, when elephants and camels were unloaded from Dunstable North station and marched up High Street and West Street.

▼ Dunstable
The Grammar School 1898

40959

The telegraph poles have appeared, along with two urchins, who judging by their dress would not have been pupils. These were not modern egalitarian levelling-down days: grammar boys wore caps or straw boaters, grey shorts and shirts and socks. Shoes were black, and the tie was short and woollen with horizontal stripes; the blazer was dark blue. The school took boarders, and was very much minor public school in aspiration.

◄ Dunstable, High Street c1955

D69005

This is an interesting contrast to picture No 39735, with the lorries out in force along this major artery for the expanding 'never had it so good' British economy. The shops are getting flashier too, but they have a long way to go to reach the millennium marvels we see today. Ladies' coats and shoes are sensible, no one is 'strutting their stuff' as they strut today. Cars are small and friendly-looking, not aggressive status symbols flashing the latest number plates or styles - but progress is on its way.

Dunstable, High Street c1964 D69025
Curry's Morris Minor van makes a bold advertisement for the nation's favourite electrical retailers. Their shop sold the latest hi-fi record players, and pop music was all the rage. The California Ballroom saw some famous names, including the local Baron Knights - a group thriving on spoof comic versions of the leading groups of the time. Cars could still park easily along the High Street. A selection of the latest types are displayed here, and also some interesting oldies like the chunky American-styled Vauxhall Wyvern, parked just beyond the traffic island. Evoking an earlier age of transport, a curious penny farthing sign hangs over a shop front.

Dunstable
High Street South c1955 D69002
The town's tree-lined streets were ideal for London overspill.
Entering the picture via West Street, left, the London Transport
AEC RT-type double decker bus service would remind
newcomers of home - except for the fact that country service
buses were painted green instead of red. Nowadays, inevitably,
these services are history.

Dunstable
High Street North c1967 D69048
Car parking is getting heavier, necessitating angled-off road parking slots and
double yellows. There is an array of popular models here, including the sought-
after Rover. Invigorated management and Peter Bache's design team produced
a model placed in Europe's top three. It was aimed at a new concept clientele:
the young executive. Sad to say, the British motor industry was heading for one
of its worst periods of industrial relations, which meant that production did not
match design - the industry was heading for decline. For the moment, all looks
very British, right down to the crown on the side of the green Morris Post
Office telephone van, parked outside the toy and cycle shop, with a neat little
circle of defensive cones to ward off the more careless driver. Hartley Carpets
occupy a typical 1960s structure, fashionable then but dull now, offering a little
luxury for the mass market of increasingly house-proud consumers.

**Dunstable
High Street c1965** D69026
We are looking south, where post-war architecture is starting to get
the upper hand. The Co-op drapers, outfitters and footwear shop is
almost opposite the stately-looking ABC Cinema; in front of it is a
'mod'-looking motor scooter and a 'rocker'-looking motor bike!
Everything looks cheerful and changing. A radical little mini-van
displays a rare A-registration plate. The status-conscious gimmick
to sell cars by advertising their age had come in halfway through
the year, so that many waited until January 1964 to get the B-
registration. This was all very British, and about 'keeping up with
the Joneses', as they put it in those days.

Dunstable, Downside Estate c1965 D69046

The name might suggest that this was some kind of down-town dumping ground for the less fortunate; but the name referred to the fine location near Dunstable downs, and the flats, houses and shops were state-of-the-art for the time. There are plenty of cars on display, including the side of a 1950s locally-built Vauxhall Velox , far right. Other features include a clattering little milk float on its busy rounds and a Corporation Leyland bus ready for return to Luton. The green foreground represents the age of idealism; there was, and still is, plenty of room to escape south into more greenery - it is really quite an upside.

Dunstable, Broad Walk c1965 D69055

Typifying the sixties town planning dream here, Broad Walk presents a range of shops away from the hazard and pollution of the motor car. The fashion for pedestrianisation can seem bland, but styles have improved since these early days. At least they faced these buildings with bricks instead of the grey and grim concrete so popular thirty-odd years ago.

◀ **Dunstable, Queensway Hall c1965** D69044
More civic architecture here in the shape of Queensway Hall in Court Drive; in line for this era of betterment, the Hall is housing an improvement grant exhibition. The sixties might have been swinging ,but there was still much poverty among the plenty, with an abundance of outside loos, dampness and hardship for children. Harold Wilson, Labour Prime Minister, was getting ready to sort it all out with his 'white-hot technological revolution'.

Dunstable
The Civic Hall c1965
D69029

This is a very different proposition to picture No 39738. It all looks very functional, and in that sense must have represented progress. But in some ways, it looks as if Captain Kirk and his crew have just entered through a time warp and have forgotten to engage the cloaking device!

Dunstable, St Mary's
Church c1965 D69033

This is a far cry from the old Priory; but it is an interesting and inspiring modern design, with an innovative approach to the old spire concept. Without the cheap labour of old, and with high maintenance costs, this is the only way to build for a church of declining popularity, which is keen to cut costs and to present a cooler image for an image-obsessed society.

Dunstable
The Chalk Cutting
1924 75583

This is the A5. Originally a Roman road, it ran here at a much higher level. The cutting was the result of Thomas Telford's improvements to help stage coaches climb from the valley bottom and negotiate down to the Bedford levels - the mail coaches went through Luton.

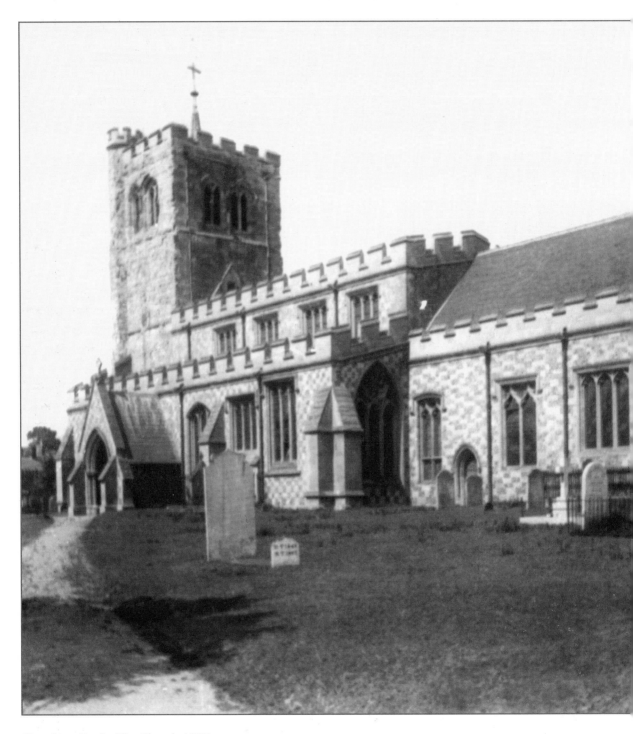

Houghton Regis, The Church 1897 39751
The church has flint and stone chequer work with early 14th-century arcades, and a carved Norman font with a fluted bowl. Anglican parsons were so hostile to John Wesley when he preached here that they refused to have the bells rung or to help him on with his gown. They thus inadvertently encouraged him to start his own church; Luton's first Methodist Hall, which was in Church Street, opposite St Mary's.

Rural Roundabout

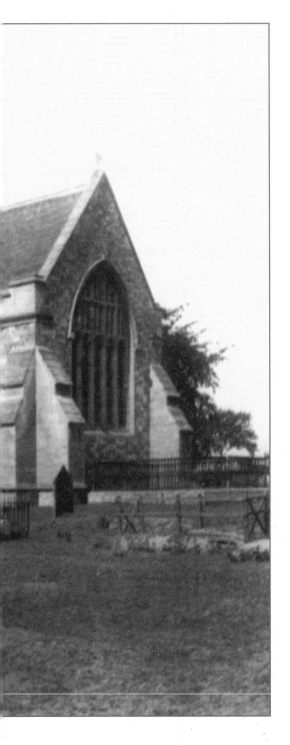

Bedfordshire is a small county, dominated by Luton, Dunstable and Bedford, but still rich in glorious countryside and villages. Francis Frith would have enjoyed a much different outlook while on his Victorian travels; but as well he knew, he was photographing a world of subtle change. Today there is fear for the future of rural life; villages are fast becoming commuter havens, with rising property prices, parking problems and a new compact style of development and architecture. But that is the price of success. It is pleasant here, and many want to share the mix of rural bliss and modern conveniences.

Houghton Regis was once a royal manor. Henry I carved Dunstable from the south of it because he wanted to establish a market. Thus the town has the rare claim of being established on a royal whim. Eaton Bray and Totternhoe were sited on the Great Moor to the south-west; they shared common land in the days when ordinary folk spent time working on their master's land by day and on their own little strips afterwards. Education was minimal; one chantry priest was paid 28s 8d a year for teaching 6 poor children. Today's Houghton is engulfed by Dunstable's spread.

Standing on a hill where five roads converge, Toddington has gone from town to village - its market was granted in 1218. From the Houghton direction, the church looks like a skyscraper out of place, for it is covered with polythene and is undergoing restoration. Its great cruciform bulk rises up over the village green. Harpenden, over the county border in Hertfordshire, has lost its village ponds and rustic feel in all but a little part, but retains something of a rural atmosphere and is a fine setting for suburban golfers. By the 1960s it was an urban district with a population of 18,278.

Going north of the Luton conurbation, we find Eaton Bray and Totternhoe between Leighton Buzzard and Dunstable and only a few miles from each. Both have been influenced by the commuter drift which has also been attracted by their near neighbour Milton Keynes, but this is still very much countryside and farmland. George Brown, nineteen years old, moved from Houghton Regis to Leighton Buzzard, buying tenancy of the forge in 1841; he was soon joined by his son William. The firm prospered along with local agriculture. After World War One, they benefited from the tractor boom. The firm has gone from strength to strength, though these days they do a fair trade selling garden tractors and lawn mowers. This again reflects the rise of affluent commuters and employees of buoyant new industries in executive accommodation. Leighton Buzzard and Linslade, famous for its links with the Great Train robbery of the sixties, have been joined since the 1940s, reflecting the earliest attractions of the area. It taxes the sharpest brains to find out how to protect the rural flavour which even newcomers enjoy whilst continuing to expand. Toddington Parish Council are among those concerned to protect their heritage. Jennifer Saunders, Parish Clerk, said: 'we are keenly aware of our history, and have a very active parish council five year plan and great pride in our village to spur us along'. There is indeed much to be proud of in this beautiful part of the Home Counties.

◄ Harpenden, The Village 1897

39730

Bearing a name meaning 'valley of the nightingales', Harpenden has an image to match in this Victorian scene. A flint and stone medieval church tower stands just off the High Street. The church, like much of today's town, dates from the last century. By 1960 this was an urban district of 18,278; today it is quite a thoroughfare, with a Sovereign bus service to Boreham Wood and a railway to London. Barbara, a retired secretary, said: 'I was one of many exiled Scots who came for jobs. I commuted to London and didn't enjoy the diesel trains. Those were the days when they used to catch fire!'

Toddington, The Green c1965 T160020
Elizabeth I was entertained here when the manor belonged to the Cheneys. The staunchly Royalist Wentworth family arrived in 1614; Lord Wentworth and his son fled to command the Royalist cavalry when war began. His grand-daughter, Henrietta, regained the title and estate after the republican interlude. Marrying the Duke of Monmouth, she sheltered him at Toddington when his scheme to take the throne from James II came unstuck. The well-kept green reminds us of great days when it was a market place for the plait trade. It now has a memorial garden in place of these railings.

Harpenden, The Village Pond 1897 39732
Railways made Victorian countryside accessible to city dwellers, and writers romanticised it so much that many moved out there. Urbanisation had begun. This was the land of town planner Ebenezer Howard's dreams. With a gorse-clad common, walks through fields and woods and a car factory just up the road in Luton, what better place for a dream come true?

Totternhoe The Hill 1897 39755
A few miles from Dunstable, through the Downs, and nowadays part of the commuter belt, Castle Hill road links the three ends of Totternhoe, Church, Middle and Lower. A pathway leads up to the castle mound which overlooks the surrounding countryside. Possibly originally a prehistoric fort, it is a motte and bailey earthwork. Totternhoe was the last Bedfordshire parish to be enclosed in 1891.

**Totternhoe
The Village 1897**
39754
This is the lower end of the village. A mother and her large Victorian family, including a baby and pram, are happy to pose for the camera - well, the girls are at least. The boys seem a little shy! Totternhoe was famous for its quarries, which supplied stone for building Windsor Castle. There was a Roman villa in Church End, opposite the church.

◄ **Eaton Bray, The Church c1955** E104009
Falkes de Breaute and William de Cantilupe built castles here. The latter was among those extorting Magna Carta from the King. The Brays came and gave the place its name in 1490. Sir Reginald became Treasurer of England, being involved in building Henry VII's chapel in Westminster Abbey. Once entirely dependent on farming , its downland location makes it an attractive settlement for more affluent newcomers, and the one-time council houses display the spirit of Thatcher-age sell-offs.

◀ Leighton Buzzard All Saints Church c1965 L211013

This fine building has a lofty spire, befitting an ancient prebend providing revenue to the Bishop of Lincoln. The suffix 'Buzzard' comes from the town's first prebendary; but since changes to the county boundary and steady growth, it would be more appropriate to call the town Leighton Linslade.

◀ Leighton Buzzard, High Street c1965 L211050

At the time of this picture, Leighton was an urban district of 11,649 inhabitants. It had a 15th-century market cross and varied light industries. These included the building of Vickers' Vimy bombers during the war, which were towed along Billington Road to a field, where the wings were attached, they were then flown off to the war. The plane factory site was later used to build the Morgan 3-wheeler.

Luton
View from the Air c1955 L117301
This aerial view shows a variety of old rooftops before the sweeping
changes that brought the Arndale Centre. The town hall makes a bold
centrepiece. The war memorial before it carries the message: 'They
gave the most that man can give, life itself for God, for King and
country, for loved ones'. It is people that make a place, and today
there is a different town, facilitated by those sacrifices.

Index

Frith Book Co Titles

www.frithbook.co.uk

The Frith Book Company publishes over 100 new titles each year. A selection of those currently available are listed below. For latest catalogue please contact Frith Book Co.

Town Books 96pp, 100 photos. County and Themed Books 128pp, 150 photos (unless specified). All titles hardback laminated case and jacket except those indicated pb (paperback)

Around Aylesbury (pb)	1-85937-227-9	£9.99	Down the Thames	1-85937-121-3	£14.99
Around Bakewell	1-85937-113-2	£12.99	Around Dublin	1-85937-058-6	£12.99
Around Barnstaple	1-85937-084-5	£12.99	Around Dublin (pb)	1-85937-	£9.99
Around Bath	1-85937-097-7	£12.99	East Anglia (pb)	1-85937-265-1	£9.99
Berkshire (pb)	1-85937-191-4	£9.99	East London	1-85937-080-2	£14.99
Around Blackpool	1-85937-049-7	£12.99	East Sussex	1-85937-130-2	£14.99
Around Bognor Regis	1-85937-055-1	£12.99	Around Eastbourne	1-85937-061-6	£12.99
Around Bournemouth	1-85937-067-5	£12.99	Edinburgh (pb)	1-85937-193-0	£8.99
Around Bradford (pb)	1-85937-204-x	£9.99	English Castles	1-85937-078-0	£14.99
Brighton (pb)	1-85937-192-2	£8.99	English Country Houses	1-85937-161-2	£17.99
British Life A Century Ago	1-85937-103-5	£17.99	Around Exeter	1-85937-126-4	£12.99
British Life A Century Ago (pb)	1-85937-213-9	£9.99	Exmoor	1-85937-132-9	£14.99
Buckinghamshire (pb)	1-85937-200-7	£9.99	Around Falmouth	1-85937-066-7	£12.99
Camberley (pb)	1-85937-222-8	£9.99	Folkestone	1-85937-124-8	£9.99
Around Cambridge	1-85937-092-6	£12.99	Gloucestershire	1-85937-102-7	£14.99
Cambridgeshire	1-85937-086-1	£14.99	Around Great Yarmouth	1-85937-085-3	£12.99
Canals and Waterways	1-85937-129-9	£17.99	Greater Manchester (pb)	1-85937-266-x	£9.99
Cardiff (pb)	1-85937-093-4	£9.99	Around Guildford	1-85937-117-5	£12.99
Carmarthenshire	1-85937-216-3	£14.99	Around Harrogate	1-85937-112-4	£12.99
Cheltenham (pb)	1-85937-095-0	£9.99	Hastings & Bexhill (pb)	1-85937-131-0	£9.99
Around Chester	1-85937-090-x	£12.99	Helston (pb)	1-85937-214-7	£9.99
Around Chichester	1-85937-089-6	£12.99	Herefordshire	1-85937-174-4	£14.99
Around Chichester (pb)	1-85937-228-7	£9.99	Around Horsham	1-85937-127-2	£12.99
Churches of Berkshire	1-85937-170-1	£17.99	Humberside	1-85937-215-5	£14.99
Churches of Dorset	1-85937-172-8	£17.99	Around Ipswich	1-85937-133-7	£12.99
Colchester (pb)	1-85937-188-4	£8.99	Ireland (pb)	1-85937-181-7	£9.99
Cornish Coast	1-85937-163-9	£14.99	Isle of Man	1-85937-065-9	£14.99
Cornwall	1-85937-054-3	£14.99	Isle of Wight	1-85937-114-0	£14.99
Cornwall (pb)	1-85937-229-5	£9.99	Kent (pb)	1-85937-189-2	£9.99
Cotswolds (pb)	1-85937-	£9.99	Kent Living Memories	1-85937-125-6	£14.99
County Durham	1-85937-123-x	£14.99	Lancaster, Morecombe & Heysham (pb)		
Cumbria	1-85937-101-9	£14.99		1-85937-233-3	£9.99
Dartmoor	1-85937-145-0	£14.99	Leeds (pb)	1-85937-202-3	£9.99
Derbyshire (pb)	1-85937-196-5	£9.99	Around Leicester	1-85937-073-x	£12.99
Devon	1-85937-052-7	£14.99	Leicestershire (pb)	1-85937-185-x	£9.99
Dorset	1-85937-075-6	£14.99	Around Lincoln	1-85937-111-6	£12.99
Dorset Coast	1-85937-062-4	£14.99	Lincolnshire	1-85937-135-3	£14.99
Dorset Living Memories	1-85937-210-4	£14.99	London (pb)	1-85937-183-3	£9.99
Down the Severn	1-85937-118-3	£14.99	Ludlow (pb)	1-85937-176-0	£9.99

Available from your local bookshop or from the publisher

Frith Book Co Titles (continued)

Around Maidstone	1-85937-056-x	£12.99	South Devon Living Memories	1-85937-168-x	£14.99
Manchester (pb)	1-85937-198-1	£9.99	Staffordshire (96pp)	1-85937-047-0	£12.99
Peterborough (pb)	1-85937-219-8	£9.99	Stone Circles & Ancient Monuments		
Piers	1-85937-237-6	£17.99		1-85937-143-4	£17.99
New Forest	1-85937-128-0	£14.99	Around Stratford upon Avon	1-85937-098-5	£12.99
Around Newark	1-85937-105-1	£12.99	Suffolk (pb)	1-85937-221-x	£9.99
Around Newquay	1-85937-140-x	£12.99	Surrey (pb)	1-85937-	
Norfolk (pb)	1-85937-195-7	£9.99	Sussex (pb)	1-85937-184-1	£9.99
North Devon Coast	1-85937-146-9	£14.99	Swansea (pb)	1-85937-167-1	£9.99
North Yorks	1-85937-236-8	£9.99	Tees Valley & Cleveland	1-85937-211-2	£14.99
Norwich (pb)	1-85937-194-9	£8.99	Thanet (pb)	1-85937-116-7	£9.99
Around Nottingham	1-85937-060-8	£12.99	Tiverton (pb)	1-85937-178-7	£9.99
Nottinghamshire (pb)	1-85937-187-6	£9.99	Around Torbay	1-85937-063-2	£12.99
Around Oxford	1-85937-096-9	£12.99	Around Truro	1-85937-147-7	£12.99
Peak District	1-85937-100-0	£14.99	Victorian & Edwardian Kent	1-85937-149-3	£14.99
Around Penzance	1-85937-069-1	£12.99	Victorian & Edwardian Maritime Album		
Around Plymouth	1-85937-119-1	£12.99		1-85937-144-2	£17.99
Norfolk Living Memories	1-85937-217-1	£14.99	Victorian and Edwardian Sussex		
North Yorks (pb)	1-85937-236-8	£9.99		1-85937-157-4	£14.99
Preston (pb)	1-85937-212-0	£9.99	Victorian & Edwardian Yorkshire	1-85937-154-x	£14.99
Reading (pb)	1-85937-238-4	£9.99	Victorian Seaside	1-85937-159-0	£17.99
Salisbury (pb)	1-85937-239-2	£9.99	Warwickshire (pb)	1-85937-203-1	£9.99
Around St Ives	1-85937-068-3	£12.99	West Midlands	1-85937-109-4	£14.99
Around Scarborough	1-85937-104-3	£12.99	West Sussex	1-85937-148-5	£14.99
Scotland (pb)	1-85937-182-5	£9.99	West Yorkshire (pb)	1-85937-201-5	£9.99
Around Sevenoaks and Tonbridge	1-85937-057-8	£12.99	Weymouth (pb)	1-85937-209-0	£9.99
Somerset	1-85937-153-1	£14.99	Wiltshire Living Memories	1-85937-245-7	£14.99
South Hams	1-85937-220-1	£14.99	Around Winchester	1-85937-139-6	£12.99
Around Southampton	1-85937-088-8	£12.99	Windmills & Watermills	1-85937-242-2	£17.99
Around Southport	1-85937-106-x	£12.99	Worcestershire	1-85937-152-3	£14.99
Around Shrewsbury	1-85937-110-8	£12.99	York (pb)	1-85937-199-x	£9.99
Shropshire	1-85937-083-7	£14.99	Yorkshire Living Memories	1-85937-166-3	£14.99
South Devon Coast	1-85937-107-8	£14.99			

Frith Book Co titles available 2001

Lake District (pb)	1-85937-275-9	£9.99	Luton (pb)	1-85937-235-x	£9.99
Sussex (pb)	1-85937-184-1	£9.99	Cheshire (pb)	1-85937-271-6	£9.99
Northumberland and Tyne & Wear (pb)			Peak District (pb)	1-85937-280-5	£9.99
	1-85937-281-3	£9.99	Dorset (pb)	1-85937-269-4	£9.99
Devon (pb)	1-85937-297-x	£9.99	Liverpool and Merseyside (pb)	1-85937-234-1	£9.99
Bedford (pb)	1-85937-205-8	£9.99	Surrey (pb)	1-85937-081-0	£9.99
Down the Thames (pb)	1-85937-278-3	£9.99	Buckinghamshire (pb)	1-85937-200-7	£9.99
Hereford (pb)	1-85937-175-2	£9.99	Heart of Lancashire (pb)	1-85937-197-3	£9.99
Brighton (pb)	1-85937-192-2	£9.99			

See Frith books on the internet www.frithbook.co.uk

FRITH PRODUCTS & SERVICES

Francis Frith would doubtless be pleased to know that the pioneering publishing venture he started in 1860 still continues today. A hundred and forty years later, The Francis Frith Collection continues in the same innovative tradition and is now one of the foremost publishers of vintage photographs in the world. Some of the current activities include:

Interior Decoration

Today Frith's photographs can be seen framed and as giant wall murals in thousands of pubs, restaurants, hotels, banks, retail stores and other public buildings throughout the country. In every case they enhance the unique local atmosphere of the places they depict and provide reminders of gentler days in an increasingly busy and frenetic world.

Product Promotions

Frith products are used by many major companies to promote the sales of their own products or to reinforce their own history and heritage. Frith promotions have been used by Hovis bread, Courage beers, Scots Porage Oats, Colman's mustard, Cadbury's foods, Mellow Birds coffee, Dunhill pipe tobacco, Guinness, and Bulmer's Cider.

Genealogy and Family History

As the interest in family history and roots grows world-wide, more and more people are turning to Frith's photographs of Great Britain for images of the towns, villages and streets where their ancestors lived; and, of course, photographs of the churches and chapels where their ancestors were christened, married and buried are an essential part of every genealogy tree and family album.

Frith Products

All Frith photographs are available Framed or just as Mounted Prints and Posters (size 23 x 16 inches). These may be ordered from the address below. From time to time other products - Address Books, Calendars, Table Mats, etc - are available.

The Internet

Already twenty thousand Frith photographs can be viewed and purchased on the internet. By the end of the year 2000 some 60,000 Frith photographs will be available on the internet. The number of sites is constantly expanding, each focussing on different products and services from the Collection.
The main Frith sites are listed below.
www.francisfrith.co.uk
www.frithbook.co.uk

See the complete list of Frith Books at:

www.frithbook.co.uk

This web site is regularly updated with the latest list of publications from the Frith Book Company. If you wish to buy books relating to another part of the country that your local bookshop does not stock, you may purchase on-line.

For further information, trade, or author enquiries please contact us at the address below:
The Francis Frith Collection, Frith's Barn, Teffont, Salisbury, Wiltshire, England SP3 5QP.
Tel: +44 (0)1722 716 376 Fax: +44 (0)1722 716 881 Email: uksales@francisfrith.co.uk

See Frith books on the internet www.frithbook.co.uk

TO RECEIVE YOUR **FREE** MOUNTED PRINT

Mounted Print
Overall size 14 x 11 inches

Cut out this Voucher and return it with your remittance for £1.50 to cover postage and handling, to UK addresses. For overseas addresses please include £4.00 post and handling. Choose any photograph included in this book. Your SEPIA print will be A4 in size, and mounted in a cream mount with burgundy rule lines, overall size 14 x 11 inches.

Order additional Mounted Prints at HALF PRICE (only £7.49 each*)

If there are further pictures you would like to order, possibly as gifts for friends and family, purchase them at half price (no additional postage and handling required).

Have your Mounted Prints framed*

For an additional £14.95 per print you can have your chosen Mounted Print framed in an elegant polished wood and gilt moulding, overall size 16 x 13 inches (no additional postage and handling required).

---

* IMPORTANT!
These special prices are only available if ordered using the original voucher on this page (no copies permitted) and at the same time as your free Mounted Print, for delivery to the same address

---

Frith Collectors' Guild

From time to time we publish a magazine of news and stories about Frith photographs and further special offers of Frith products. If you would like 12 months FREE membership, please return this form.

Send completed forms to:
The Francis Frith Collection, Frith's Barn, Teffont, Salisbury, Wiltshire SP3 5QP

Voucher for **FREE** and Reduced Price Frith Prints

Picture no.	Page number	Qty	Mounted @ £7.49	Framed + £14.95	Total Cost
		1	**Free of charge***	£	£
			£7.49	£	£
			£7.49	£	£
			£7.49	£	£
			£7.49	£	£
			£7.49	£	£

Please allow 28 days for delivery	*** Post & handling**	**£1.50**
Book Title	**Total Order Cost**	**£**

Please do not photocopy this voucher. Only the original is valid, so please cut it out and return it to us.

I enclose a cheque / postal order for £ . . . . made payable to 'The Francis Frith Collection' OR please debit my Mastercard / Visa / Switch / Amex card *(credit cards please on all overseas orders)*

Number . . . .

Issue No (Switch only) . . . . .Valid from (Amex/Switch) . . . .

Expires . . . . Signature . . . .

Name Mr/Mrs/Ms . . . .

Address . . . .

. . . .

. . . . Postcode . . . .

Daytime Tel No . . . .   Valid to 31/12/02

The Francis Frith Collectors' Guild

Please enrol me as a member for 12 months free of charge.

Name Mr/Mrs/Ms . . . .

Address . . . .

. . . .

. . . . Postcode . . . .

Free Print - see overleaf